# 5 MINUTE:

## Teacher-Tested

# LEARNING GAMES

Emmi S. Herman

This edition published in 2001.

Interior Illustrations by: Doug Cushman

ISBN: 0-8167-2581-0

Printed in the United States of America.

10  9  8  7  6  5

# ⟨ CONTENTS ⟩

## Science

## Music and Movement

## Old Favorites

# INTRODUCTION

Classroom games can be stimulating, creative, and a lot of fun! In *5-Minute Teacher-Tested Learning Games* there are over 110 games and activities that are simple enough to learn quickly yet interesting enough to play again and again. All of the games can be set up and played in a few minutes in a limited space.

The games in this collection are grouped by content area: Language Arts/Spelling, Math, Social Studies, Science, and Music and Movement. Traditional games are also included in the section called Old Favorites. In each content area, the games progress in difficulty level. Many games contain suggestions for variations, which are helpful in making adjustments for levels of skill.

## PANTOMIMING WORDS

**P**repare index cards with an adjective (*worried, angry, excited, nervous, frightened, brave,* or *silly*) written on each. Ask a volunteer to come to the front of the room, choose a card, and pantomime the adjective that is written on it. Have the class guess the word. The player who guesses correctly becomes the next pantomime artist!

## TELEPHONE

**T**his oral language and listening game is played in a circle. The leader thinks of a sentence and whispers it in the ear of the player to the right. That player whispers what he or she hears to the next player. Play continues until the last person repeats the sentence out loud to see if it matches the original sentence. Caution: This game may have hilarious results!

# GROUPIES

To play this categorizing game, have players gather in groups that have a common interest. For example, favorite ice-cream flavor, color of shoes, birthday month, or favorite TV show. As players sort and group themselves, they will have fun learning about one another.

# OLLIE, OLLIE, OLLIE-ED!

**T**his rhyming game is a good way to have children line up for lunch, yard, or dismissal. Sing the following rhyme to children:

Ollie, Ollie, Ollie-*ed*!
Get on line if you're wearing *red*.

Vary the word endings at the end of the first line. For example, *een* for *green*, *ink* for *pink*, and so on. As a variation, leave out the last word of the last line and have one child supply a rhyming word. Continue play until all the children are in line.

## SILLY STORIES

**B**egin a story with *Once upon a time*. A player then adds a silly phrase. Continue the story and have another player add another silly phrase, and so on. Play may go clockwise in a circle or you may point to different children randomly. For example:

Teacher: Once upon a time . . .

Player 1: a green monster came to my house . . .

Teacher: It asked me . . .

Player 2: for gooey monster food . . .

## KNOCK, KNOCK, KNOCK ON THE DOOR

**T**he leader recites a line to the other players, who give different rhyming responses. The rhyme may go like this:

Leader: Knock, knock, knock on the door.

Player 1: Come right in and sweep the floor.

Leader: Knock, knock, knock on the door.

Player 2: Let me in, said the wind with a roar.

## I'M PACKING MY SUITCASE

**B**egin this listening game by saying "I'm packing my suitcase with a shirt." One player repeats your word and adds one that begins with the sound *sh* as in *shirt*. The game continues until a player cannot repeat the previous words in the correct sequence or cannot give a new word that begins with *sh*.

## I'M GOING TO ALASKA

**T**his alliteration game is played in a circle. Each player is assigned a letter of the alphabet and has to make up a sentence using as many words as possible that begin with that letter. Players go in alphabetical order. Begin with "I'm going to . . ." and name a place and a reason. For example:

Player 1: I'm going to Alaska to announce another award.
Player 2: I'm going to Bolivia to borrow blue balloons.
Player 3: I'm going to Canada to collect colorful curtains.

## ⟨ WRITE IT DOWN ⟩

The object of this small group activity is to write names of objects that begin with the same letter within a certain amount of time. Assign one player in each group to record the answers for the group. Write a letter on the chalkboard and set a five-minute time limit. Remind players to keep their voices low so that the groups do not hear one another. The group with the most names written after the time limit is up wins. As a variation, specify that names be animals, flowers, or countries.

B
bike
balloon
bird
bear
barn

B
bell
banana
bush
basket
basketball

B
bee
bunny
ball
blouse

# THE PERFECT SEQUENCE

**D**ivide the class into small groups. Give each child a sequence of directions to follow, such as "Hop on your left foot, sit on your chair, put your head on your desk." "Write the number 5 on a piece of paper, add 1, divide by 3, and add 3." Award points to each group that follows directions correctly.

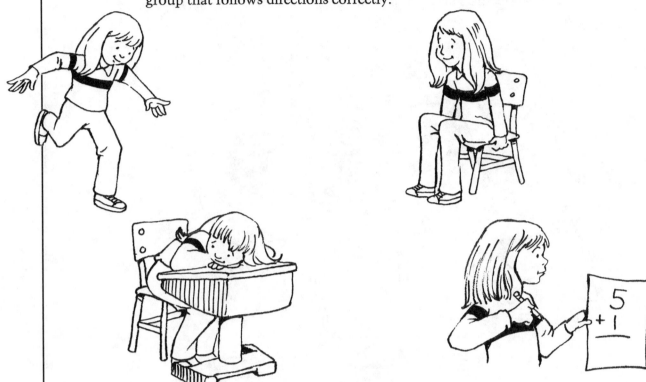

# A HORSE OF A DIFFERENT NAME

**C**reate new animal names by combining two names or parts of animal names into one. For example, a hen and a pelican become a henican, a horse and an antelope become a horselope. List the new animal names on the chalkboard. Have children illustrate their new animals.

# LET'S MAKE WORDS

This activity may be played in groups of six to eight. Write the letters of the alphabet on index cards and give a card to each player, allowing for fair distribution of vowels and difficult letters, such as *z*, *x*, and *q*. Have each group form as many words as possible from their letters. Have groups share their results with the rest of the class.

# CHANGE A WORD, CHANGE A SENTENCE

For this game, children play in a circle. The object is to pass a sentence from player to player, changing one word at a time. Write a sentence on the chalkboard. The first player reads the sentence; the next player says the sentence but changes one word. Players substitute verbs for verbs, nouns for nouns, and so on. Verify with the class that each new sentence makes sense. Continue until all players have a chance to contribute a word and change the sentence.

## ⟨ WORDS WITHIN WORDS ⟩

**T**his game trains the eye to see smaller words within a larger word and increases vocabulary. Write a word on the chalkboard, such as *teacher*, and have children write down all the smaller words they find in the word. *(teach, each, ache, her, tea)* As a variation, form as many words as possible by rearranging the letters. *(For example: earth, car, tar, hear, reach, heart, cheer, cheat, heat, tear, ear, chart)*

## ⟨ CONCENTRATION ⟩

**H**ave the class sit in a circle and copy a pattern such as: tap knees twice, clap hands twice, snap fingers twice. Keep the pattern going as you say the following:

Concentration is the name of the game.

Are you ready? Let's go!

Start with kinds of animals.

At the beginning of the pattern a different kind of animal is named. Designate who will go first, and the game moves clockwise. If an animal name is not given at the beginning of the pattern, or if a name is repeated, the game starts over. The purpose of the game is to complete the circle by naming a different animal without breaking the pattern.

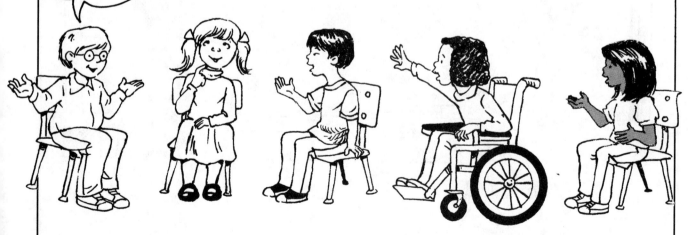

16

# WORD PICTURES

Children may work in small groups or individually to create word pictures. A word picture uses the letters of a word to illustrate its meaning. *Hot* may be drawn with wavy lines over the *o* to show heat, and *nail* may be drawn with a nail head at the base of *l* to look like a carpenter's nail. Have a brainstorming session, after which children illustrate their own word pictures.

# SYNONYM HUNT

**H**ave children think of synonyms for words such as *round, tall, short, big,* and *little.* Assign groups for each word and have them write the words on chart paper. Save the lists for use in creative writing.

# WHAT'S RED?

**T**his creative thinking game may be played in large or small groups. Have children brainstorm things that are red and record them on chart paper. Follow the same procedure for several other colors. Save the lists for later use in writing descriptive sentences.

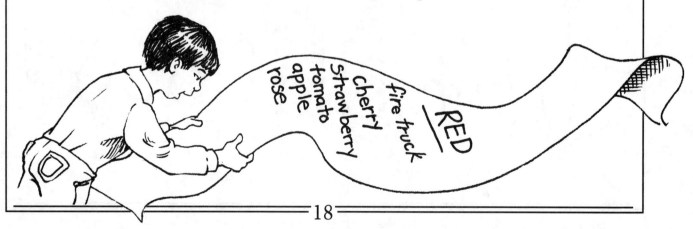

Children love tongue twisters, and this activity gives them the chance to make up their own! Use your own name as an example, such as: Ms. Elton eats eleven elephants every evening. Encourage children to be creative and silly.

Ms. Elton eats eleven elephants every evening.

# YOU'VE GOT PERSONALITY

**D**istribute paper and pencils and ask students to write a short description about themselves that makes them unique. Encourage students to write about their likes, dislikes, experiences, and accomplishments. Collect the descriptions and redistribute in random order. Have each student read the description and ask the rest of the class to figure out who wrote it.

I like to feed the class gerbils.

I can play the piano.

# SAY IT AGAIN

**G**ive each player a slip of paper with a simple sentence written on it. Have players read their sentences aloud in the following ways:
1. As if they were running and out of breath
2. As if they didn't understand the sentence
3. As if it were the funniest thing they ever heard
4. As if they were frightened
5. As if they were sad

# REVERSE MY NAME

**H**ere's a quick and fun activity that adds new interest to children's names. Have children write their full names on pieces of paper. Then, on other pieces of paper, have children reverse the spellings. Point out any names that remain the same when reversed. Collect the reverse spellings and redistribute them at random. Call on a volunteer to pronounce the reverse name aloud and have the class guess the correct name. Verify the answer with the correct spelling. The person who guesses correctly goes next.

MOT REKLAW

ANNOD ENAL

ANNA EROOM

YRREP NOTTUS

EEL OTON

ARAM DLEIF

# NAME GAME

**D**istribute index cards, scrap paper, and pencils. Have children print their names with the letters in mixed-up order. Collect the cards and redistribute them. Have children use scrap paper and pencil to unscramble the anagram names.

# WORD ASSOCIATION

**F**or this categorizing activity, write several headings across the tops of pieces of chart paper. Headings might include *Fairy Tales, Scientists, Authors, Movies,* and *Music*. Name a heading and ask a player to write a word or name associated with it. Continue play until each player has had a turn. Ask a volunteer to record the responses on the chart paper and add to the list as the year goes on.

| Fairy Tales | Authors | Movies |
|---|---|---|
| Red Riding Hood | Steven Kroll | An American Tail |
| The Three Bears | Bernard Waber | The Bear |
| Cinderella | Eric Carle | Duck Tales |
| Thumbelina | Judy Blume | Home Alone |
| Rapunzel | Arnold Lobel | Batman |
| Snow White | Maurice Sendak | Teenage Mutant Ninja Turtles II |
| The Little Prince | Cynthia Rylant | |
| Three Little Pigs | Uri Shulevitz | |
| Sleeping Beauty | Beverly Cleary | |

**D**ivide the class into two teams and a panel of judges to play this cause-and-effect game. Write a simple cause-and-effect statement on the chalkboard, such as *If I watch too much television, then my mother will ground me.* Distribute pencils and paper to all and ask one team to write *If* phrases and the other to write *then* phrases. Encourage students to write creatively and refer them to the chalkboard if necessary. After students are finished writing, ask a player from the *If* team to read an *If* phrase out loud, followed by the word *silly* or *serious.* The *then* team quickly decides which of their phrases would complete a silly or serious statement. If the response satisfies the panel of judges, the *then* team scores two points and that team starts the next round. The first team to score twenty points wins.

If I plant these seeds...

then tomatoes will grow.

# GO-TOGETHERS

Prepare a list of things that commonly come in pairs. For example, shoes and socks, cup and saucer, pencil and paper, salt and pepper, thunder and lightning, king and queen, bacon and eggs, hot dog and bun. On slips of paper write the names of one of the objects in each pair and pin those slips to the backs of the players so that they do not know the words they are wearing. After all the players are pinned, they must ask questions to find their mates. In order to do so, they must first find out their own identities by asking each other questions, such as "Am I an animal?" Continue play until all have found their mates.

**H**ave children create their own abbreviated telegrams by giving initial letters only. Write several letters on the chalkboard, such as *S W S B S B M.* Ask volunteers to create a telegram from the given letters. (The example could be: Sent wrong size blouse. Shipping back Monday.) Continue by writing different sets of letters on the chalkboard for which children will create other telegrams.

# CHALKBOARD RELAY

**D**ivide the class into two or three teams of equal numbers and assign portions of the chalkboard to each. The first player in each team races to the chalkboard, picks up the chalk, and writes the first word of a sentence. He or she runs back, hands the chalk to the next player in line, and that player runs to the board and continues the sentence by writing the second word. Play continues until the sentence is finished. The first team to complete a sentence without any mistakes is the winner.

# ONE POTATO, TWO POTATO

To play this counting game, have players sit in a circle and hold their fists out in front of them. Choose a leader to tap each fist as the children chant:

> One potato, two potato, three potato, four.
> Five potato, six potato, seven potato more!

When a fist is tapped on *more*, that child puts one fist behind his or her back. Play continues until only one child has a fist held out and is declared the winner.

# WHO STOLE THE COOKIES?

This counting and sequencing game may be played with children sitting in a circle on the floor. Choose a player to be Player 1. In a clockwise direction, assign consecutive numbers to the other players. Have children chant both as a group and alone when their number is called:

> Group: Who stole the cookies from the cookie jar?
>    Player One stole the cookies from the cookie jar!
>
> Player One: Who me?
>
> Group: Yes you!
>
> Player One: Couldn't be.
>
> Group: Then who?
>
> Player One: Player Two stole the cookies from the cookie jar!

Continue play until all players' numbers have been called. As a variation, have players call numbers out of sequence to keep everyone alert.

# HOW MANY FINGERS?

As a warm-up activity, flash your fingers in front of children and have them tell how many you hold up. You may begin slowly, holding up ten fingers and putting down one finger at a time.

Distribute large white paper, pencils, and crayons. Help children trace their hands on the paper. Tell them to choose a number from 1 to 10 and write the numeral at the top of the paper. Then have them color the number of fingers that match the numeral they wrote.

# SHAPE UP!

This game of recognizing simple geometric shapes may be played individually or in small groups. Draw the following shapes on the chalkboard: circle, triangle, large rectangle, small rectangle, and square. Write a numeral inside each shape. Tell children to draw a specific object using shapes you indicate by number. For example, ask them to draw a truck using four number 1's, one number 2, and one number 3. If played in small groups, set a time limit. The group that draws the object first using all the correct shapes is the winning team.

# BIRTHDAY FUN

Children love to celebrate birthdays, and this activity may be played after a birthday snack. Say the following rhyme aloud with the children:

> January, February, April, May,
> When will it be your birthday?

Point to a player after the word *birthday* and have the player tell his or her birthday month. Repeat the rhyme with that player pointing to another to give his or her birthday month. Continue play until all children have participated. As a variation, when a player gives his or her birthday month, all players sharing that birthday month stand up until another month is named.

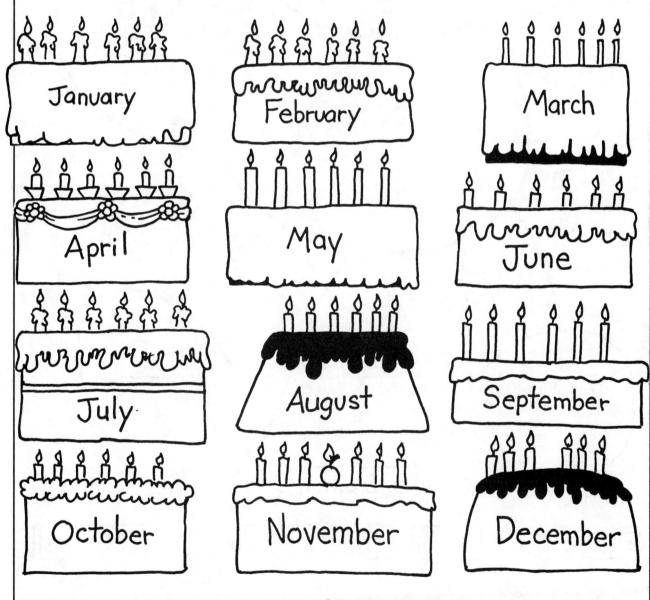

# ADDITION BEAR

Add and color.

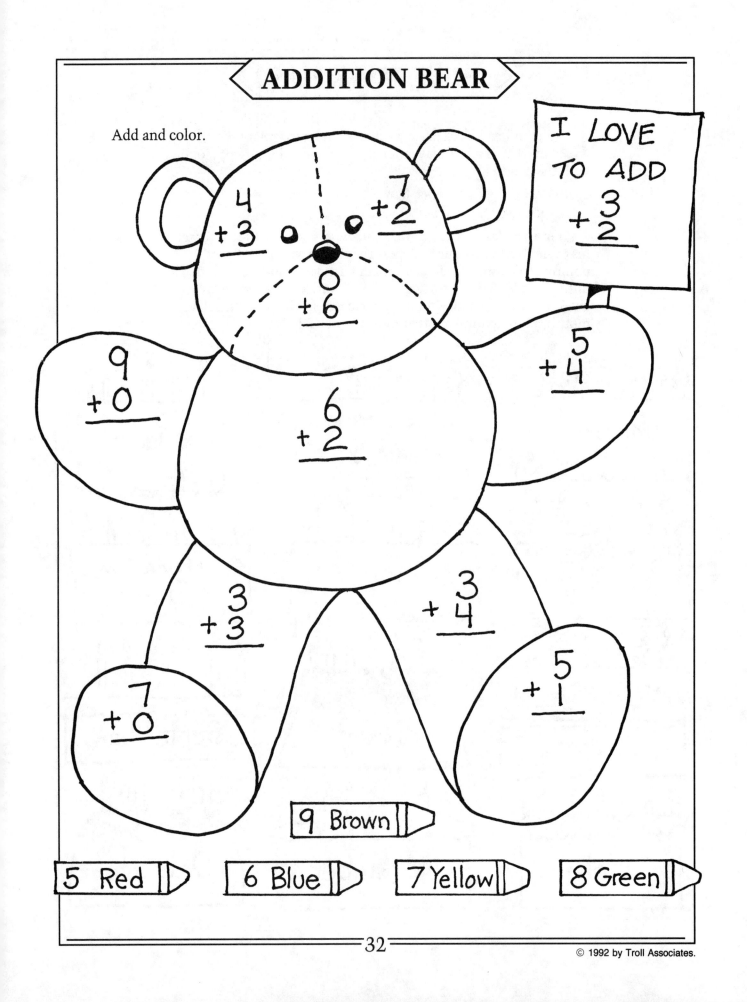

I LOVE
TO ADD
$$\begin{array}{r} 3 \\ +2 \\ \hline \end{array}$$

$$\begin{array}{r} 4 \\ +3 \\ \hline \end{array}$$

$$\begin{array}{r} 7 \\ +2 \\ \hline \end{array}$$

$$\begin{array}{r} 0 \\ +6 \\ \hline \end{array}$$

$$\begin{array}{r} 5 \\ +4 \\ \hline \end{array}$$

$$\begin{array}{r} 9 \\ +0 \\ \hline \end{array}$$

$$\begin{array}{r} 6 \\ +2 \\ \hline \end{array}$$

$$\begin{array}{r} 3 \\ +3 \\ \hline \end{array}$$

$$\begin{array}{r} 3 \\ +4 \\ \hline \end{array}$$

$$\begin{array}{r} 7 \\ +0 \\ \hline \end{array}$$

$$\begin{array}{r} 5 \\ +1 \\ \hline \end{array}$$

9 Brown

5 Red    6 Blue    7 Yellow    8 Green

32

## ⟨ IN A FLASH ⟩

**U**se arithmetic flash cards for this game. Divide the class into two teams and have them line up on opposite sides of the room. Assign the members on one team numbers that correspond to the numbers on the other team. Show a flash card and, after a few seconds, call out a number that has been assigned to the teams. The first child to answer the flash card problem correctly wins a point for his or her team.

## ⟨ MAD MONEY! ⟩

**P**lay this game in small groups. Each group should have play money of various denominations. Write an amount of money using the dollar sign and decimal point on the chalkboard. Have children show the amount using the play money. Point out different combinations for the same money amount. The first child called on who has the correct answer may write the next money amount on the chalkboard.

# MATH BINGO!

**M**ath Bingo is a variation that helps to sharpen addition and subtraction facts. Distribute a standard bingo card to each player. Choose a caller, who begins by giving an addition or subtraction problem. Choose a recorder, who writes the problem on the chalkboard. Players figure out the answer, find it on their bingo cards, and cover it with a marker. If they do not find the answer on their cards, they wait for the next problem. The first player to cover his or her card horizontally, vertically, or diagonally wins. Verify answers by checking the problems on the chalkboard.

# NUMBER LINE

**P**repare numeral cards using 1- to 3-digit numbers. Divide the class into two teams and have teams face each other. Then distribute to each player one numeral card, in random order and facedown. Tell players to line up in numerical order when you say "Go!" and to shout "Number line!" when the entire team is placed. The first team that lines up in the correct numerical order gets two points. Then collect cards and repeat above procedure. The first team to get 10 points wins the game.

# HIGH-FLYING NUMBERS

Find the differences and connect the dots.
Color the picture.

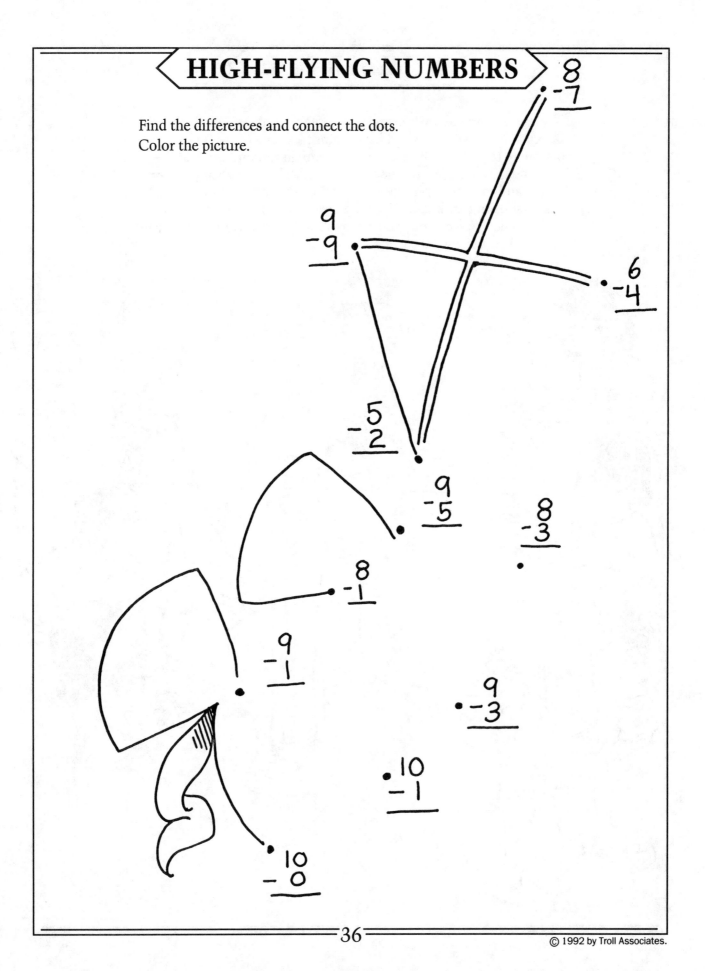

$$\begin{array}{r} 8 \\ -7 \\ \hline \end{array}$$

$$\begin{array}{r} 9 \\ -9 \\ \hline \end{array}$$

$$\begin{array}{r} 6 \\ -4 \\ \hline \end{array}$$

$$\begin{array}{r} 5 \\ -2 \\ \hline \end{array}$$

$$\begin{array}{r} 9 \\ -5 \\ \hline \end{array}$$

$$\begin{array}{r} 8 \\ -3 \\ \hline \end{array}$$

$$\begin{array}{r} 8 \\ -1 \\ \hline \end{array}$$

$$\begin{array}{r} 9 \\ -1 \\ \hline \end{array}$$

$$\begin{array}{r} 9 \\ -3 \\ \hline \end{array}$$

$$\begin{array}{r} 10 \\ -1 \\ \hline \end{array}$$

$$\begin{array}{r} 10 \\ -0 \\ \hline \end{array}$$

# SKYWRITING NUMBERS

This game may be played as a large-group activity or in teams. One player comes up to the front of the class and stands with his or her back to the group. With exaggerated motions, the player "skywrites" a numeral high in the air for the rest of the players to observe. When another player correctly identifies the numeral, he or she becomes the next skywriter. As a more challenging variation, have players skywrite addition and subtraction problems for the rest of the players to solve.

# THE SECRET NUMBER

The object of this game is to trick a player into saying a secret number before that player guesses the number. To begin, choose a player to leave the room. The rest of the class then agrees on a number. When the player returns, the class has five minutes to ask questions that will make the player say the secret number as many times as possible. The class should ask general questions that don't give away the number. For example, if the secret number is 12, the class might ask, "How old will you be in the seventh grade?" Meanwhile, the player must figure out the secret number based on the questions being asked. He or she should wait until the five-minute period is over before guessing the number.

## SET THE CLOCK

This activity is a hands-on method of telling time. Prepare strips of oaktag showing various times and place the strips facedown on a desk. Display a clockface along the chalk ledge. Call on children, one at a time, to select a strip, read the time, and set the clock to show that time. Continue until all children have had a turn.

## TIME TO MATCH

This game may be played by two to four players. Prepare a set of cards with clockfaces showing various times. On another set of cards, write the time shown on each clockface. Mix the cards and place them facedown. Players take turns matching a clockface with the correct time. If a player makes a match, he or she takes a turn again. The player with the most matches wins.

# BODY NUMBERS

This activity adds a new dimension to the concept of numbers. Choose three players to come up to the front of the class. Tell them a number quietly so that the rest of the class doesn't hear. Have them use their bodies to form the number. For example, to form number 107, one player stands erect with arms down to form a 1, the next player faces sideways and touches his or her toes without bending knees to form a 0, and the last player stands erect with one arm raised at shoulder height to form a 7. You may assist players in manipulating their bodies to form the number. Ask the rest of the class to tell the number. The first child who correctly states the number gets to form the next number with two or three other players of his or her choice. As a variation, have two players use their bodies to form one number.

# CROSS NUMBER PUZZLE

Find the sums or differences and complete the puzzle.

**Across**

A. $289 + 27 =$ _____

D. $57 + 11 =$ _____

E. $911 - 268 =$ _____

F. $65 + 74 =$ _____

J. $799 - 54 =$ _____

K. $897 - 69 =$ _____

**Down**

A. $845 - 809 =$ _____

B. $9 + 9 =$ _____

C. $326 + 423 =$ _____

F. $306 - 289 =$ _____

G. $196 + 152 =$ _____

H. $999 - 47 =$ _____

I. $636 - 535 =$ _____

# MEASURE UP!

Have children play in small groups for this game of estimation. Prepare twenty-four index cards with pictures of objects with linear shapes, such as a pencil, pen, book, fork, spoon, and knife. Measure each pictured object and on the back of each card, write the measurement to the nearest half inch. Each child chooses a card and guesses the length of the pictured object. Then have the child verify his or her guess by checking the back of the card. If the guess is correct, the player keeps the card. The player with the most cards at the end of the game wins.

# BASEBALL MATH

Divide the class into two teams and assign a "batting order." Designate areas in the classroom for first, second, and third bases and home plate. Choose a team to be up first. "Pitch" simple addition, subtraction, multiplication, or division problems to the player at bat. If the player answers correctly, he or she moves to first base, and the next player is up. As players answer correctly, they move around the bases to make a home run. If the player answers incorrectly, he or she is out and goes to the end of the line. After three outs, the next team is up. It is important to pitch questions quickly to keep the game going. As a variation, have players from the team that is not at bat pitch the problems. The team with the most runs after three innings wins.

# CALCULATOR GAME

Divide the class into two or three groups. Prepare several series of 2- and 3-digit multi-step number problems on a piece of paper. Give each group a calculator. Say the first number in the series and have the first player in each group enter the number into the calculator. Pass the calculator to the next player to compute (add, subtract, multiply, or divide) the next number. Players continue computing and passing the calculator to find the answer to the problem. Remind players to press the add, multiply, subtract, or divide key when necessary. Verify answers and give two points to each group that gets the correct answer. The group that gets ten points first wins.

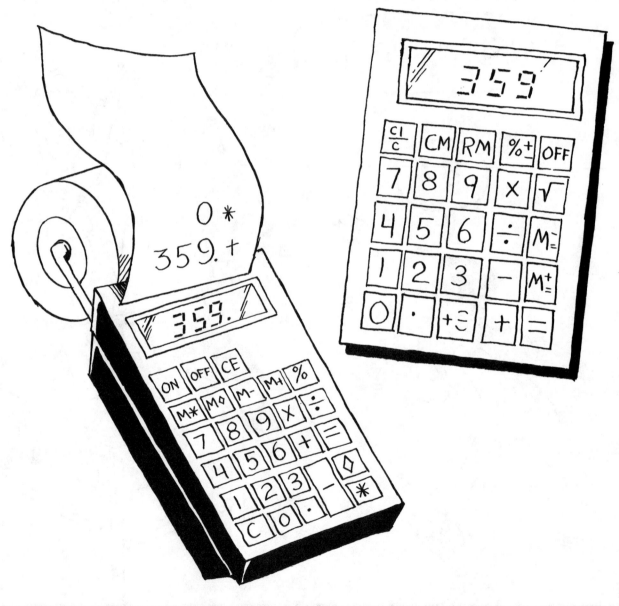

# IF I HAD ONE HUNDRED DOLLARS . . .

Distribute paper and pencils to children and tell them to imagine that they were just handed one hundred dollars to spend any way they want. Have them list the ways they would spend the money and write the dollar amount next to each item. Remind children that the items on their lists must add up to exactly one hundred dollars—and not a penny more!

If I had $100
Compact Disc
for Todd-$12.00

Sweater for
Mom $25.00

# GEOMETRIC SCULPTURE

1. Color the pattern.
2. Cut out the pattern along the solid line.
3. Fold along the dotted lines.
4. Glue corresponding tabs and sides to finish your geometric shape.

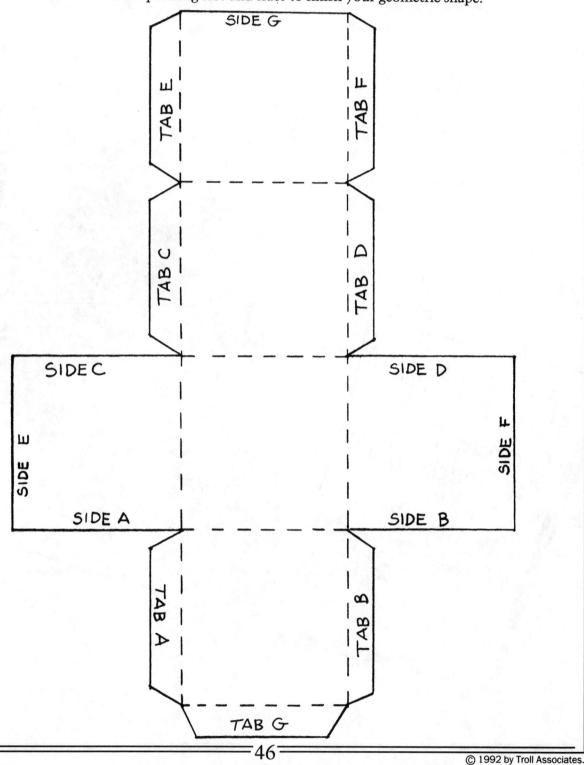

# SAD, SCARED, GLAD GAME

In this game players pantomime different emotions. To make sure players are familiar with the words for different emotions, have volunteers give examples of things that make them *happy, sad, excited, worried,* and so on. Ask players to pantomime different emotions. As a variation, have players pantomime an emotion and ask the class to identify it.

# SAME, DIFFERENT

This game shows that although everyone is unique, we all have something in common with other people. Have children form a circle. Assign a leader to call out a characteristic that describes a person, such as blue eyes, black hair, or something more specific such as curly brown hair or bangs. Have players who fit the description come to the center of the circle. Verify the common characteristic and have children return to their places. Have the leader call out the next characteristic. Continue to play until all children have come to the center of the circle at least once.

# SAME GAME

Collect pairs of items that are alike in some way, such as chalk, eraser; sock, shoe; pencil, marker; spoon, fork; pillow, blanket; ball, block; paper, workbook; and so on. Put all items in a carton. Call on a volunteer to select two items from the carton and display them. Have the group tell what is the same about the two objects. Encourage children to think about weight, color, shape, size, and purpose of objects when giving their answers. Call on another volunteer and repeat the procedure. As a variation, ask children to tell what is different about the two objects.

## SCHOOL JOBS

**H**ave children brainstorm the types of jobs people have in school, such as teachers, principal, assistant principal, secretary, custodian, nurse, guidance counselor, librarian, cook, and security guard. Then choose a player to go out of the room and choose a school job to assign that player. When the player returns, he or she must guess the job by asking questions, such as "Do I work in the office?" When the player guesses correctly, another player goes out of the room and the process is repeated.

## SCHOOL TALK

**H**ave children improvise a dialogue to resolve school situations such as the following:

1. Principal talking to a parent about a child's misconduct
2. Nurse helping a child with an injury
3. Teacher helping a student understand a lesson
4. Cook planning the menu with a food supplier
5. Child telling a classmate about having chicken pox

# TRAFFIC SIGNALS GAME

This traffic safety rules game may be played as a large-group activity. Choose one child to be the police officer. Ask the rest of the children to pretend that they are driving vehicles. Have them line up on a starting line, about twenty feet away from the police officer. When the officer calls out "Green light," the vehicles move forward. When the officer calls out "Yellow light," the vehicles proceed slowly, and when "Red light" is called, all vehicles stop. Any vehicles moving when "Red light" is called must return to the starting line. The child who reaches the police officer first becomes the next caller. As a variation, have the police officer give instructions by holding up traffic-light signs of green, yellow, and red.

# SHOPKEEPER, SHOPKEEPER, WHAT DO YOU SELL?

In this large-group activity, players think of things sold in the store whose names begin with a given letter. Choose a shopkeeper and a letter of the alphabet. The game proceeds like this:

All players: Shopkeeper, shopkeeper, what do you sell?

Shopkeeper: I am a shoe store owner, and I sell things that begin with the letter s.

Player 1: You sell sandals.

Player 2: You sell sneakers.

Player 3: You sell socks.

Player 4: You sell slippers.

Play continues until children cannot think of any more items. Begin a new round with a new shopkeeper and a new letter.

# FAMOUS PERSON MATCH

In this small-group game, players match the names of famous people with their occupations. Prepare one set of index cards with names of famous people and another set with titles, such as president, author, explorer, inventor, scientist, astronaut, and so on. Mix the cards and place them facedown on a table or desk. Players take turns matching the name of a famous person with his or her occupation. The player with the most pairs wins the game. As a variation, prepare one set of index cards with occupations and another set with job descriptions, such as *oceanographer* and *person who studies underwater life.*

# GREAT INVENTIONS

For this activity, children become inventors of gizmos and gadgets. Have them brainstorm devices that would help them perform a task, such as a sandwich maker or a room-cleaning robot. Then distribute drawing paper and crayons and have children draw their inventions. Have them write the names of their inventions at the top of their papers. Call on volunteers to tell about their inventions and explain how they work. After each presentation, encourage the audience to ask questions and comment on the invention.

# WHAT'S IN A NAME?

On the chalkboard or on chart paper, prepare a list of famous inventors or explorers whose names have become synonymous with a place or product, such as Amerigo Vespucci (America), Louis Braille (Braille printing), Zebulon Pike (Pikes Peak), Louis Pasteur (pasteurization). Divide the class into two teams and have players think of a word originating from each famous name. Set a time limit of five minutes. Award one point for each name. The team with the most points wins.

Sandwich . (n) named after the Fourth Earl of Sandwich (1718-92) for whom sandwiches were made so that he could stay at the gambling table.

# SLOGAN MANIA

It is a good idea to begin this activity by discussing a school or community issue that the children feel strongly about. Help them focus on how they may help to improve a situation. Then ask children to write snappy slogans, such as:

Don't Delay—Recycle Today!

A Cleaner Tomorrow Can Be Yours If You Recycle Today.

Be Smart . . . and Recycle It.

# THE POWER OF ADVERTISING

Put in a box several objects commonly found in the classroom, such as chalk, pencil eraser, paperback book, and highlighter pen. Have pairs of children come up to the front of the class and choose one product to sell on television. Give them a few minutes to prepare their commercials. Ask the rest of the class to be consumers and vote by secret ballot whether or not they would buy the product based on the commercial. Tally the results and announce the winning copywriters!

# WHAT'S MY CAREER?

This is a guessing game. Have children pantomime careers that interest them. To prepare children, remind them to think of what tasks are involved, how the person would dress and move, and the types of tools that the person would use. Give children a few minutes to prepare their pantomime before getting up in front of the class.

# I WISH FOR THE WORLD . . .

Name famous people who have acted on their good wishes for others, such as Martin Luther King, Jr. and Golda Meir. Give each child an opportunity to make up a good wish for the world.

 I wish for the world that all the people have enough food to eat.

# KNOCK ON WOOD

Choose one player to be "It." While the rest of the players close their eyes, It knocks three times on an object in the room. When It returns to the front of the room, the players open their eyes and guess the object that It knocked. The player who guesses correctly becomes the next It.

# THE BUBBLE GAME

In this activity children first blow imaginary bubbles to form their own space, and then end up as one giant bubble. Have players form a circle. Ask them gently to blow a bubble all around themselves to create any size bubble. Make sure they move carefully so that don't "break" their bubbles. Then have players join hands to make one big bubble. Ask the bubble to float, twirl, sink, and pop!

# WHO SWIMS?

**F**or this activity, make sure all the players have plenty of room to move around. Begin by saying "Ducks swim," and have all players imitate a swimming motion. Continue the swimming motion and ask, "What else swims?" Point to a player to give an answer, such as "Fish swim. What else swims?" and that player points to another to give an answer. If a player names an animal that does not swim, everybody says "Stop" and imitates the correct motion of the animal named. For example, if a player says "Cats swim," everybody says "Stop" and imitates a cat walk. Continue the game by asking "What else walks?"

Ducks Swim!

# EARTH, WATER, AIR

**P**repare twenty colorful flash cards of different kinds of animals. As you show each picture, players shout out "Earth" or "Water" or "Air" to name the element with which the animal is associated. For example, if a picture of a bear is shown, players shout "Earth." More than one element may be associated with an animal. Allow time for players to explain their answers.

# THE FIVE SENSES GAME

In this activity, players are asked to use one of their five senses in an imaginary place. Prepare oaktag cards with a symbol for one of the five senses on each. Distribute a card to all players. Have them look at their "sense" cards and concentrate while you describe an imaginary place. Ask players to tell about the imaginary place using only the sense given on their cards. For example, if the imaginary place is *campground at night,* a player with a hearing card might say *leaves rustling, mosquitoes buzzing.* Give all players an opportunity to respond to each imaginary place. Have players exchange sense cards before starting a new round. Other imaginary places may include the fish store, a crowded bus, the ocean, a train, the zoo, and the playground.

# LIGHTNING, THUNDER, AND A RAINBOW

**H**ere are three quick experiments related to weather that children will enjoy doing right in the classroom.

### Make Your Own Lightning

**You will need:** metal doorknob, hair comb, wool or fur

**What to do:** Have children rub the comb with a piece of wool or fur and then hold the comb near a metal doorknob. Watch as a small spark is produced.

**Why:** When the comb is rubbed, it becomes charged with electricity. The spark is made when the charge jumps to the uncharged doorknob. This is called static electricity.

### Home-Blown Thunder

**You will need:** a balloon or paper bag

**What to do:** Help children blow up the balloon or paper bag and tie it with a rubber band or piece of string. Tell them to place one hand on the top and one hand on the bottom of the bag and pop it. You hear a small clap of thunder!

**Why:** Thunder is caused by a small amount of fast-moving air. An object produces sound when it moves rapidly back and forth or up and down.

## Make Your Own Rainbow

**You will need:** a sunny window, a glass of water, a sheet of white paper

**What to do:** Put a glass of water on a window ledge in bright sunlight. Place the sheet of white paper on the floor. Have children watch as a beautiful rainbow appears!

**Why:** Various colors make up white light. When light passes from the air through the glass of water, the sun rays change direction—they become refracted. Each color bends differently, so when the light comes out of the glass of water, the different colors travel in slightly different directions and hit the sheet of paper at different places.

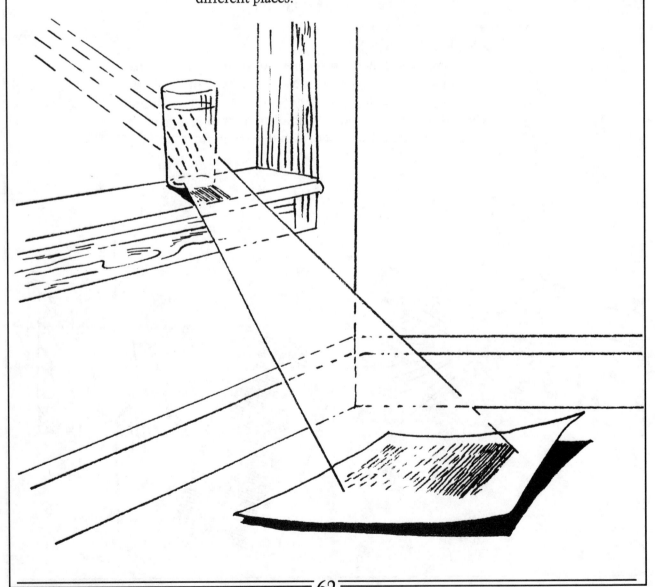

# READY, SET, FLY!

**D**istribute white sheets of paper to children. Have them make folds as shown in the pictures. Designate an area in the classroom as the "runway" and have children fly their creations one at a time. Discuss the results. Depending on the age of the group, discuss the principles of lift, thrust, drag, and gravity. Encourage children to improve on their original designs. Hold contests for "the most original design," "the longest flight," or "the highest flight."

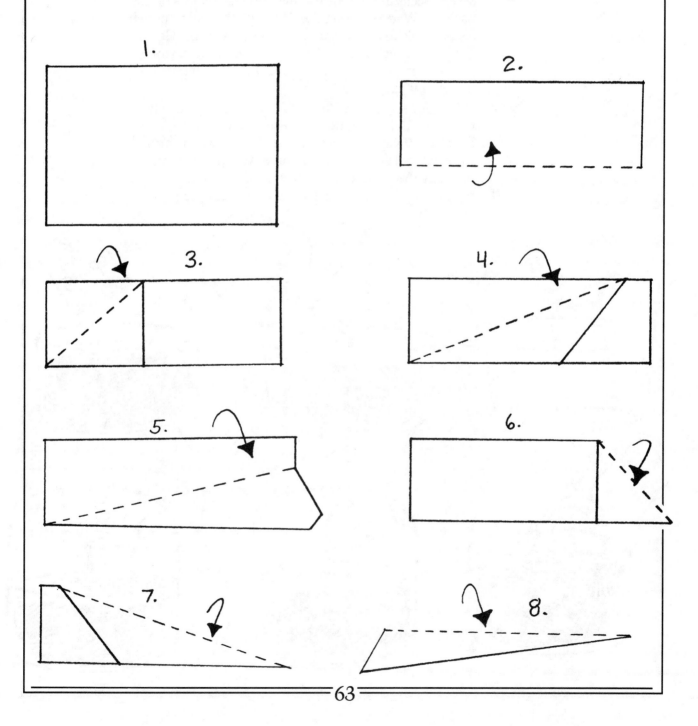

# FIVE-MINUTE TERRARIUM

**A**lthough this is a quick and simple activity for children, it is necessary to prepare some things ahead of time.

**You will need:** bottom halves of 2-liter plastic beverage bottles (two halves per child), clear or green; dirt; water; vegetable seeds; nail; clear tape.

**What to do:** Fill one of the bottle bottoms halfway with dirt. Plant several seeds in the dirt, following the directions on the package. Water thoroughly. Then use the nail to punch a small hole in the bottom of the second bottle. Cover the hole with clear tape. Fit the second bottle bottom over the first one to form a dome. Place the terrarium in a sunny place.

**Result:** Watch for sprouting! Check the terrarium often. The top part will look cloudy because it is filled with droplets of water. If necessary, add more water through the small hole on top of the dome. When the plants outgrow the terrarium, remove the dome. Water regularly, allowing the plants to continue their growth.

# SCIENCE-OLOGY

**D**ivide the class into two teams. Explain that *-ology* at the end of a word means "the study or science of." On the chalkboard write the following words as examples: *biology, microbiology, zoology, archaeology, hematology,* and so on. Ask the teams to list as many words as they can think of that end with *-ology*. Set a time limit for them to do this. Teams may use the dictionary to verify all words and write brief definitions. Award points for correct words.

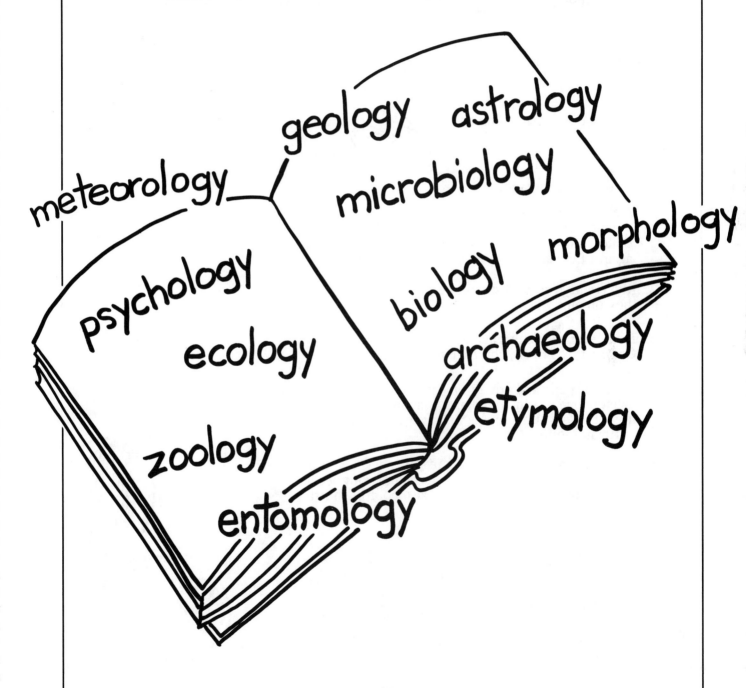

# MAKING A COMPASS

## You will need:

a dish of water

a steel needle, 2 inches (5 cm) long

horseshoe or bar magnet

thin cork with groove

iron pins and other small iron objects

## To make a compass:

1. Make the needle into a magnet by rubbing it on one end of the magnet. Rub the needle in one direction only from the center to the end of the magnet, holding it horizontally against the magnet.

2. Rub twenty times. Test your needle magnet by picking up the iron pins.

3. Float your needle magnet on the cork in the dish of water. Once it floats freely, you have made a compass.

4. Hold a magnet and other iron objects near your compass. What happens? Once you take away the magnet and other iron objects, your compass will always end up pointing north and south.

5. Compare your compass with a regular pocket compass. Find north on the regular compass. The end of your needle pointing in that same direction is also pointing north.

# WHERE IS THUMBKIN?

Have players begin by putting their hands behind their backs. Ask them to sing along and act out the finger play. As the first "Here I am" is sung, players show the appropriate finger on one hand. On the second "Here I am," the corresponding finger on the other hand is shown. During the next two lines, fingers wiggle as if they are talking to each other. For the last line, the fingers run away behind the backs again. Continue play for the other fingers: Pointer, Tall One, Ringer, Pinky.

Where is Thumbkin?
Where is Thumbkin?
Here I am. Here I am.
How are you today, sir?
Very well, I thank you.
Run away, run away.

# HEAD, SHOULDERS, KNEES AND TOES

This is a wonderful stretching activity to help start the day or to use as a transition from one activity to another. Make sure children have space to stretch. As they sing, have them use their hands to point and bend toward body parts.

Head, shoulders, knees and toes, knees and toes;
Head, shoulders, knees and toes, knees and toes;
Eyes and ears and mouth and nose;
Head, shoulders, knees and toes, knees and toes.

Continue play, increasing the pace of the song and thus the movement, with each round. As a variation, have children sing:

Hair, elbows, hips and thighs, hips and thighs;
Hair, elbows, hips and thighs, hips and thighs;
Brow and cheeks and tongue and chin;
Hair, elbows, hips and thighs, hips and thighs.

# PERSONALIZED "LOOBY LOO"

**H**olding hands, the players form a circle. Have them walk to the right as they sing the personalized chorus of "Looby Loo" as shown below. When that chorus is finished, the players stop walking, but continue to sing and follow the directions in the second stanza, as dictated by the named player.

Here we go [any player's name].
Here we go Looby Light,
Here we go [(same) player's name].
All on a Saturday night.

I put my two hands in,
I put my two hands out,
I give my two hands a shake, shake, shake,
And turn myself about. Oh!

## POPCORN KIDS

This large-group activity will help children release excess energy. Have children crouch on the floor, pretending to be little kernels of popcorn. Slowly, as you say "Pop. Pop pop," the kernels begin to pop up and down. Soon all players are hopping as they become popped popcorn. Choose one player to "eat" the popcorn. As he or she touches each popcorn, the popcorn sits down.

## VEGETABLE PAIRS

In this large-group activity, assign one player to be a chef and pairs of players to be a single vegetable. Have pairs disperse and sit in chairs in a circle while the chef stands in the middle. The chef calls out the name of a vegetable. The two players whose vegetable is called get up and switch chairs while the chef tries to sit in one of the vacated chairs. The player left standing becomes the new chef, and the chef becomes the vegetable. As a variation, the chef calls "tossed salad" and *all* players switch seats. The player left standing becomes the new chef.

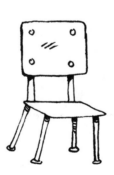

# I'M A LITTLE TEAPOT

Tell all players to pretend that they are teapots. As they sing the first line of the song, have them stand tall, place one hand on hip to make the handle, and extend the other arm with elbow and wrist bent. During the second line, have them exaggerate the handle position. During the third line, have them exaggerate the spout position. On the last line, players tip sideways to pour the tea.

(1) I'm a little teapot short and stout,
(2) Here is my handle,
(3) Here is my spout,
(4) When I get all steamed up then I shout,
(5) Tip me over and pour me out.

# MAGIC MOTION

In this large-group activity, players follow the movement of the person directly in front of them to create a rippling effect. Have players line up. The leader begins a motion that is passed down the line. For example, if the leader raises his or her arms to shoulder height, the second person in line follows the leader, the third person in line follows the second, and so on. The movements are made by arms and legs raising, bending, and twisting, rather than by moving around the room. As a variation, divide the players into two lines and have the second leader mirror the movement of the first leader.

# MOTHER, FATHER, MAY I?

Assign one child to be the mother or father and the rest of the players to be the children. While children stand approximately 20 feet (6 m) away from the mother or father, he or she calls out to one player to take any number of steps. For example, the mother or father says: "Susan, you may take three baby steps." Susan responds, "Mother, may I?" Mother replies, "Yes," and Susan takes three baby steps. If a player forgets to say "Mother, may I?," he or she must go back to the starting place. Encourage children to create unusual steps or movements such as butterfly flutter, elephant walk, or karate jump.

# DID YOU EVER SEE A RABBIT?

This song and movement game is sung to the tune "Did You Ever See a Lassie?" Have children form a circle. Choose a player to be the Rabbit and have him or her stand in the center of the circle. Have the rest of the class walk around the Rabbit while singing the song. During the fourth line, the Rabbit hops or jumps. After the sixth line, the players stop and copy the action. At the last line, the Rabbit points to another player to be the performer. As a variation, have children dramatize favorite characters, such as Teenage Mutant Ninja Turtles, Peter Pan, Alice in Wonderland, and so on.

(1) Did you ever see a rabbit,
(2) A rabbit, a rabbit?
(3) Did you ever see a rabbit
(4) Go this way and that?
(5) Go this way and that way,
(6) Go this way and that way,
(7) Did you ever see a rabbit
(8) Go this way and that?

# BALLOON RELAY

**D**ivide the group into two teams and have players line up, one behind the other. Place a chair about 10 feet (3 m) in front of each team. Have players place a balloon between their knees and hop to the chair, around it, and back to the starting point. Have them hand the balloon to the next player in line. Players may touch the balloon only when handing it to a teammate or to pick it up when it drops. The first team to complete the relay wins.

# CLUCK, CLUCK, CLACK, CLACK

Have players sit in a circle on the floor, with their legs crossed and their knees touching their neighbors' knees. Sing the tune of "Old MacDonald Had a Farm" with players, replacing the song's words with "cluck, cluck" and "clack, clack." Repeat the song several times until everybody learns it. Then begin adding movements. On the "cluck, cluck," players clap hands twice; on the "clack, clack," they gently slap the knees of the neighbor to the right. Repeat this movement pattern for the entire song. Have players gently sway back and forth once they feel comfortable with the hand movements. As a variation, substitute other tunes, such as "B.I.N.G.O.," "Home on the Range," and so on. Encourage players to develop their own movement patterns.

# A SOUND ORCHESTRA

Here is a chance to transform your group into an orchestra. Decide on simple hand gestures to refer to specific sounds. For example, raising a hand might mean "hiss," clenched fists might mean "yap," and so on. When the group can make three or four sounds in rapid succession when given the gestures to do so, choose a player to conduct the sound orchestra. Tell the player to add gestures to suggest loudness and softness. As a variation, divide the players into groups for each sound.

# FREEZE DANCING

For this large-group activity, make sure players have an unobstructed space in which to dance. A radio or a record player serves as a good source of music. Tell players to dance, move, or sway while the music is playing and to freeze as soon as the music stops. It is a good idea to keep the music source hidden so that players rely on their ears and not their eyes to know when to stop dancing. Players who move after the music stops must sit down. The last player to remain standing wins.

# PLAY DOUGH

For this activity, pairs of children work together to maneuver their bodies into creative positions. Divide the class into pairs. One member of each pair will be the sculptor and the other will be the clay. Ask the sculptors to mold their clay by carefully bending their partners' arms, legs, waist, and so on. Remind the "clay" to maintain the positions in which they are molded. Set a time limit for finishing sculptures. Have each sculptor tell about his or her work of art. Then continue play by having pairs switch roles.

# HUMAN PUPPETS

**H**ave players form pairs. Tell one player to sit or stand behind the other. The player in front places his or her arms behind his or her back, while the player in back substitutes his or her arms by extending them to the front through his or her partner's arms. As the player in front begins speaking, the player in back makes appropriate gestures, as if he or she were using the front player's arms and hands. The more exaggerated the gestures, the funnier the routine. Have players imitate an orchestra conductor, a police officer, a piano player, a chef, and a typist with appropriate music or sound effects.

# WORDS AND RHYTHMS

Words have a natural rhythm. For instance, the word *please* lends itself to a slow, slithery movement while *peanut butter* suggests a marching rhythm. In this small-group activity, players demonstrate rhythms to a favorite poem, song, or short story as it is read aloud. Have groups of two to four players work together on a composition to present to the rest of the class. Assign players words and phrases. Remind them to act out the rhythm of the word rather than the meaning. One player may read the piece as the others move to the rhythms of the words.

# MIRROR GAME

**T**his activity is played in pairs. Ask one player to make subtle moves and have the partner mirror each move. After pairs have had a few minutes to practice, ask them to perform their mirror acts for the class. Ask the group to observe which player in the pair is leading. With a skilled pair, it should be difficult to tell!

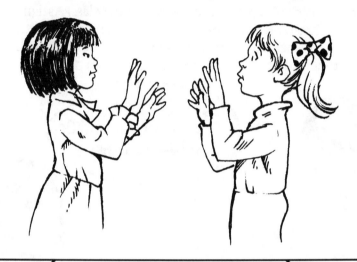

# IN PLAIN SIGHT

**I**n this large-group activity, children walk around the room in any direction and choose one person to observe without letting him or her know it. Encourage the players to move without talking and to fill in any empty spaces to prevent the group from going in only one direction. Tell players they must figure out who is watching them and at the same time, keep an eye on the person they're observing.

# FROM FLOWER SEEDS TO GENTLE BREEZES

**T**his is a perfect way to end the day. In this large-group activity, players act out their own interpretations of what the leader is suggesting. Make sure children have plenty of room to move and give them time to change from one suggestion to another. Call on a volunteer to read aloud the following passage:

We are all very small flower seeds. . . . There is rain falling on us. . . . It makes us start to sprout. . . . Our legs are becoming roots . . . our arms are becoming stems and leaves. . . . We are reaching for the sun. . . . It feels so warm on us. . . . Slowly we start to change. . . . We are little gusts of wind. . . . We are getting stronger and stronger. . . . We are now great gusts of wind in a very big storm. . . . The storm has reached its peak. . . . Slowly we are becoming calm, gentle breezes.

# FIVE-MINUTE AEROBICS

**D**ivide the class into groups of five or six. Tell players to pretend they are aerobics experts on television shows and that they must create original routines. Assign a leader and have each group practice a routine using upbeat music. Set a five-minute time limit for the routines. Have each group perform its aerobics workout. Encourage the audience to participate.

**T**his favorite children's movement game may be played by imitating animal actions. Have players form a circle. Name an animal and have the group sing the song using that animal. As they sing, tell children to imitate actions of the animal. Continue play by naming different animals.

We put the cat in,
We take the cat out,
We put the cat in,
And we shake all about.
We do the Hokey-Pokey,
And we turn ourselves about.
That's what it's all about.

# LARGER THAN A NOSE

**T**his variation of "Bigger than a Bread Box" may be played by children of all ages. Ask one child to think of something in the room that is "larger than a nose, but smaller than a face." After the child decides on an object, the rest of the players ask questions and try to guess the object based on the answers.

# HOT OR COLD

**I**n this game, a player goes out of the room while the rest of the class hides a predetermined object, such as a beanbag or chalkboard eraser. When the player comes back, he or she is guided by the word *hot* when nearing the hidden object or by the word *cold* when going away from the hidden object. Have children exaggerate saying "hot" or "cold" when the player is very close to or very far away from the object.

# DUCK, DUCK, GOOSE

**H**ave the group sit in a circle. Choose a player to be It. It walks around the circle, gently tapping each player on the head and saying "Duck." When It taps a player on the head and says "Goose," the tapped player gets up and runs around the circle trying to tag It before It sits in the vacated spot. If the player does not tag It, he or she becomes It.

## SEVEN UP!

Choose seven players to come to the front of the classroom. Ask the rest of the children to put their heads on their desks with one of their fists extended. The seven players move quietly around the room, tapping the fists of seven children. Then the seven return to the front of the room and announce "Seven up!" Those children tapped stand up and get one guess as to who tapped them. If a child guesses correctly, he or she exchanges places with the tapper. If a child does not guess correctly, the player remains a tapper for the next round. Keep the action going quickly and quietly, making sure each child is tapped at least once.

## MUFFIN MAN

**H**ave players form a circle with one child standing in the center with his or her eyes closed. The players circle to the right as they sing "The Muffin Man." When the song is over, they stop, and the child in the center walks forward, touches the player directly in front of him or her, opens his or her eyes, and says, "Yes, I see the Muffin Man. It's (name of child)." The child who is named then goes in the center.

Oh, have you seen the muffin man,
The muffin man, the muffin man?
Oh, have you seen the muffin man,
That lives in Drury Lane?

# MUSICAL CHAIRS

For this game you will need a source of music and a chair for each player less one. Arrange the chairs in a line, alternating seats and backrests. To begin, have all players march around the chairs while the music is playing. When the music stops, players quickly sit down. The player left standing is out of the game. Remove one chair and continue play. Players are not allowed to touch the chairs with their hands as they march. The last player to sit in the remaining chair wins.

# HO HUM GAME

In this game, the leader hums a song that is familiar to the players. Help leaders select songs from such categories as television show theme songs, movies, patriotic songs, or school favorites. When a player recognizes a tune, he or she raises a hand and tells the song title. If the player is correct, he or she becomes the next leader.

# SIMON SAYS

This party-game favorite is a lot of fun when played at a rapid pace. The leader calls out "Simon says do this!" and coordinates it with a specific body action, such as touching his or her head. The players, who are standing up and facing the leader, imitate the motion. If the leader says "Do this" without saying "Simon says," the players do not duplicate the motion. Those who do must sit down. The last player to remain standing is the winner and the new leader.

# MEMORY GAME

Gather six to eight small objects that have something in common, such as tape, glue, paper clips, thumbtacks, safety pins, push pins, straight pins, and stapler. Display objects on a large tray. After giving players about fifteen seconds to look at the objects, cover them with a sheet of paper. Have players write down the names of the objects that they remember seeing on the tray. As a variation, display objects that do not have a common theme. For a challenge, add more objects after each turn.

## BUZZ

Have players form a circle and tell them that they will count off to 100. This game sounds simple enough, except that every time the number 7 or a multiple of 7 comes up, the player must say "buzz" instead of the number. For example, 1-2-3-4-5-6-buzz-8-9-10-11-12-13-buzz. The object of the game is to reach 100 without making a mistake. If one person forgets to say "buzz," then the counting begins all over again.

## NUMBER RUN

This is a variation of "Upset the Fruit Basket" and uses 2- and 3-digit numbers instead of fruits. Ask one player to be the Caller and assign numbers to each of the other players. Tell the Caller to call two numbers. The two players assigned to those numbers exchange seats quickly before the Caller can get into one of the vacated seats. The player remaining without a seat becomes the next Caller.

# CHARADES

Have a volunteer come up to the front of the class and think of a title to a movie, book, or television program. Tell the volunteer to act out the words in the title, cautioning him or her not to speak. For instance, for *The Secret Garden*, the word *secret* could be acted out by putting the pointer finger to one's lips. The word *garden* could be acted out by picking flowers and waving one's arms as if to display an entire garden. Prepositions and other small words may be acted out using the thumb and pointer, motioning the sign "a little bit." When the audience figures out words correctly, the child pantomiming the title touches his or her nose and nods "yes." The first player to give the whole title correctly acts out the next title.

# FAVORITE PENCIL GAMES

**H**ave children put on their thinking caps for two old but delightful games. Players need pencils, paper, and a partner/opponent to tackle the following activities.

## SAY THE WORD

**A** player thinks of a word and writes it on a piece of paper hidden from his or her opponent's view. On another piece of paper, the same player writes dashed lines for each letter of the secret word. The object is for the opponent to guess the word by asking if it contains specific letters. The opponent should guess the word in as few tries as possible. Each correct letter is printed on the appropriate dashed line. For each incorrect guess, a stick figure is drawn, one body part at a time. This variation of the game Hangman differs in the figure that players draw: On the first incorrect guess, a head is drawn; second incorrect guess, stick body; third, stick limbs, one at a time; last, a dunce cap. Of course, no one wants to end up with a dunce cap!

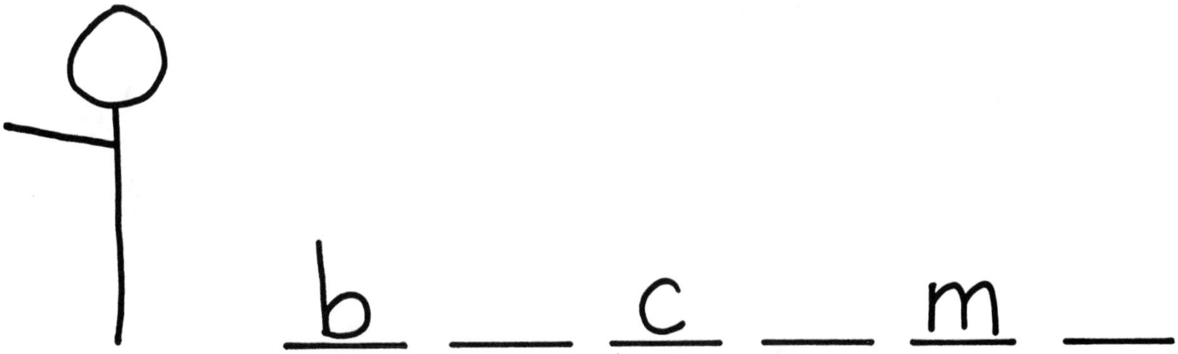

b __ __ c __ __ m __ __

# BOXED IN

Have players prepare a grid of dots similar to the one in the picture. Use one grid for each pair of players. Players take turns connecting two dots to make one line segment. The object is to make *complete* squares. The player who completes the square puts his or her initial in the box. The person who has initialed the most boxes after the entire grid is filled wins.

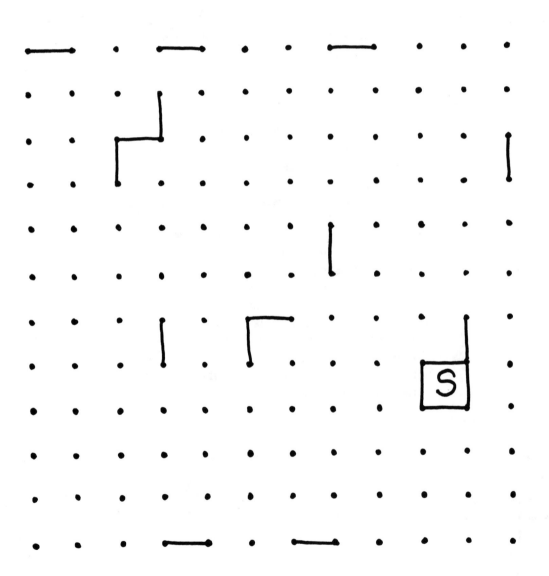